# Cultivating Contentment

# Cultivating Contentment

*Growing
through
life's
challenges*

PRESENTED BY

*Jill Briscoe*

NexGen™ is an imprint of
Cook Communications Ministries, Colorado Springs, Colorado 80918
Cook Communications, Paris, Ontario
Kingsway Communications, Eastbourne, England

CULTIVATING CONTENTMENT
© 2003 by *Just Between Us* magazine

First Printing, 2003
Printed in the United States of America

1 2 3 4 5 6 7 8 9 10 Printing/Year 07 06 05 04 03

This book is part of a series on relevant issues for today's Christian woman.
For more information on other titles in this series or for information about *Just
Between Us* magazine, please turn to the back of this book.

Library of Congress Cataloging-in-Publication Data


Cultivating contentment : growing through life's challenges / [edited by] Jill
Briscoe.
    p. cm. -- (Just between us)
  ISBN 0-7814-3952-3 (booklet : pbk.)
  1.  Christian women--Religious life. 2.  Contentment--Religious
aspects--Christianity.  I. Briscoe, Jill. II. Series.
  BV4527.C83 2003
  248.8'43--dc21
                                            2003006662

# contents

# A Note from Jill Briscoe

Dear Friends,

You will notice the special emphasis of this book is *contentment*. Statistics show that a large percentage of ministry wives don't like what they do! If there is that much discontentment, there is no question there will be discontented spouses as well. We cannot go *cold* as Christians without lowering the temperature of everyone else around us.

Discontented believers do not encourage unbelievers to believe! They do not excite believers to develop an exuberant faith. What's more, discontentment shows, and that's not good. You can't hide unhappiness of soul. You may be going through the motions of ministry because you know how to do it, but if there's no joy, there's not much hope of infectious multiplication in evangelism or spiritual growth in the church. What can we do to find contentment in ministry? Let's use an acrostic.

**C**onfess your discontentment. Paul said, "learn to be content" in Philippians 4. And confession is a good place to start.

**O**rder your private life. Check your priorities, talk them over with your partners or close friends.

**N**ourish your relationships. Do you have a friend who can encourage and challenge you? Will she call you on your discontented attitude?

**T**ry counting your blessings, not your troubles! Counting "a blessing a day keeps the devil away!"

**E**xpect the devil to whisper discouraging things in your ear. Answer him with words of Scripture— like Jesus did (Matt. 4).

**N**urture your prayer life. This is where the battle is won.

**T**rust God. Let resentment go. Forgive your enemies (and your friends). Accept adversity cheerfully. Don't play God!

How can a child of the King have a sour face? Live royally. It's your birthright.

In His Joy,

*Jill Briscoe*

# chapter one

# The Content of
# *Contentment—*
# A Christian Virtue

Reflections on Philippians 4:10-13

*Jill Briscoe*

*"I rejoice greatly in the Lord that at last you have renewed your concern for me. Indeed, you have been concerned, but you had no opportunity to show it. I am not saying this because I am in need, for I have learned to be content whatever the circumstances. I know what it is to be in need, and I know what it is to have plenty. I have learned the secret of being content in any and every situation, whether well fed or hungry, whether living in plenty or want. I can do everything through him who gives me strength."*

*I*n his book *Celebration of Discipline*, Richard Foster says, "The modern hero is the poor boy who purposely becomes rich, rather than the rich boy who voluntarily becomes poor! Hoarding we call prudence, greed we call industry. Owning is an obsession in our culture. We are all fascinated with the lives of the rich and famous. Wealth, we are told, is the benchmark of achievement. It does not seem to be a question of how much character you have—but rather how much cash!"

The best things in life are free. Let's face it: Christian people are not always content with the best things God gives us freely to enjoy. In fact, someone has convinced us if something is free, it can't be worth much! What do material things matter if your husband has walked out on you, your child is on drugs or in a bad marriage, or your health packs up? The idea that Christ can satisfy us without things our materialistic society insists are necessities for true fulfillment is for most of us only a theory anyway. As Mother Teresa said, "You can't really say 'Christ is all I need' until Christ is all you've got!" She had first-hand experience. Which of us has honestly been in that position?

The nearest I have been to this state of affairs was twenty-five years ago when the church called us to America and asked us to sell and come, as the song puts it, "just as I am." I didn't think this would be a problem for me until I had to do it. We came to the United States with two suitcases apiece—one for clothes and one for anything else we wanted to bring that would fit into one suitcase. To my spiritual chagrin, I found it very hard. It wasn't so much the valuables—very few—but rather, the nostalgic items, wedding presents, etc. It was a good reminder to all the family that Christ is the content of contentment.

The trouble is, we are led to believe by the media that we can only be content with an hour-glass figure, a gorgeous boyfriend, or a handsome mate who buys us a Hollywood house and fills our lives with exciting dates and vacations, a substantial bank balance, and a trouble-free life.

## A Christian Grace

F.B. Meyer says, "Contentment is pre-eminently a Christian grace." He cites Cicero who was always talking about courage and manly virtue, but when trouble came, complained so much he wore out his friends. And then there was Seneca, whose teaching was full of talk of stoic endurance, but who filled the air around him with abject complaints when he was exiled from Rome.

## Bound for Joy

Meyer points out the contrast of Paul, the Apostle, who was in far worse trouble than those great teachers. He was imprisoned in his last days, stripped of every comfort we take for granted, and chained to a guard, and yet he was able to say he was quite content! Deprived of his freedom and possibly facing lions or sword, Paul put down words that centuries later shout with such superb serenity, I am riveted to the text. Especially, I would have to say, when I am in trouble. After all, most of us are not looking for contentment when all is well with our world and our soul, but when all is ill with both.

When the Apostle wrote Philippians 4, he was, humanly speaking, in the saddest part of his career. Yet, as my husband puts it, "prisoner though he was, he was 'bound for joy!'" Paul found the secret of happiness was not in his circumstances, but in the loving God who had permitted those circumstances to happen. Paul was concerned the Philippians might think he was dependent upon their generous gifts for contentment and peace. He wanted them to know that in *every* situation Christ would help him to maintain an attitude of trust and confidence in Him.

## The *Content* of Contentment Is Christ

As far as Paul was concerned, the content of contentment was Christ. He said "For to me, to live is Christ and to die is gain" (Phil. 1:21). He really didn't care very much what happened to him—not because he had given up hope or was depressed or suicidal, but because he counted both options (life or death) as wonderful. It's hard to hurt a man with such a powerful perspective. It's called contentment. But I notice to my relief that this grace, this virtue, can be learned. Paul says, "I have learned in whatever state I am, to be content" (4:11, NKJV). We are enrolled by a loving God in the school of hard knocks and expected to learn our lessons well. We can all be home-schooling ourselves in the art of being content.

## The School of Hard Knocks

When my husband was on the road for months at a time, loneliness was my teacher, and I found God quite sufficient for my many lonely "nows." When I wore out trying to be both mom and dad to our three lively kids, perseverance taught me endurance and, strangely enough, gave me a settled sense of stillness that couldn't be jolted even by the most unpleasant surprises that were definitely not on my agenda.

I remember putting my children to bed one night in England. My husband was in Australia—literally on the other side of the world. He wasn't coming home for three long, hard months. My father had been diagnosed with cancer, my daughter had fallen and broken her arm the day my husband left, and my hands were more than full running a preschool, and programs for dozens of teenagers. (During this time it didn't help to catch mumps from my kids either!) Yet unbelievably, sitting by the crackling fire in our tiny home, a huge sense of well-being invaded every corner of my heart. I could hardly stand it. My heart was singing and my soul was dancing. I was content.

I have learned to accept what He allows, and change what He empowers me to change, and that's usually my attitude. I try to turn to Christ to meet my needs be they physical, relational, or spiritual. He has always come through for me.

Years ago I stopped looking to anyone else but God to satisfy me. There is no man that can love me enough, no child that can need me enough, no job that can pay me enough, and no experience that can satisfy me enough. Only Jesus. The compass of my life must be set in His direction and by His direction, and then it will, like a real compass, not be affected by motion.

## Be in the Will of God

We must be in the will of God to be content. When you believe you are exactly where God wants you to be, you wouldn't be happy if you were anywhere else in the whole wide world. When we have no complaint with His workings in our lives, we are held together inside. In fact the dictionary defines contentment as "to hold in, contain together."

What's going on inside you? Are you holding together or are you falling apart? When we are "content" with the choices God makes for us, we can respond rightly to suffering in all its shades and shadows. In other words, when we say a loud YES to God's decisions for us, we will find ourselves content.

It has often been hard for me to glance heavenward and say "aye" to God's plans and purposes in missions and evangelism that necessitated my husband's long absences, for instance, but when I learned the language of a willing and submissive heart, oh, how the peace came!

### Be in the Word of God

So to be content, we must determine to be in the will of God. Second, we must be in the Word of God and refuse to listen to Satan's dark and sinister suggestions. Satan wants to confuse us as to the matter of contentment. The Word of God will help us to think straight about our dreams, which may never materialize, or about the greed need inside us. The Scriptures, for example, may remind us "one's life does not consist in the abundance of the things he possesses" (Luke 12:15, NKJV). Paul was happy enough with what he had, and didn't desire one thing more or less to feel complete. So first we must accept the will of God for us. Second, we must refuse to listen to Satan, and instead bathe ourselves in Scripture. And third, we must decide to be more concerned with the concerns of God than with our own.

> ### LifeLifters
>
> "*O*ur contentment disappears when we let our hearts and minds be filled with self-pity and sadness, which our problems create in us. Contentment comes from recognizing how valuable our life is to God and to others."
>
> —Soula Isch—

## Be a Witness for God

By constantly applying the cross to his ambitions, murmurings, and his tendency to complain, Paul determined to look on the bright side and set himself to think of others worse off than himself. Paul knew how to be full or empty, rich or poor, rejected or accepted, loved or hated, followed or opposed, beaten or bathed and bandaged, stoned or worshipped, clothed or stripped naked, safe or in peril, tired out or well rested, burdened or light. He was even, believe it or not, content to be either dead or alive! He was willing for all or nothing as long as God was there and God was using him. Paul, full of the Spirit, gave God full permission to use him to His glory, and with that he was content whatever the repercussions.

The word used in Philippians 4 for "abased" denotes a voluntary acceptance of lowly station, even poverty, for Christ's sake. Some have suggested Paul was disinherited upon his becoming a Christian (1 Cor. 4:10-13; 2 Cor. 6:10). When things were chaotic or he suffered loss, Paul experienced Augustine's "tranquillity of order," because he was looking for ways to use the situation to lead people to Christ, not to make things more comfortable for himself.

For example, the jailers he was chained to got to hear the Gospel. After all they were a captive audience! It makes you wonder who was the prisoner. Paul believed with all his heart that his present problems were the will of God for him and so prison or no prison, fetters or no fetters, "the things that had happened to him were falling out to the good of the Gospel," and he was very happy about that.

Contentment is finding the strength we need to accelerate the progress of the Gospel—even when we are sitting in jail. Paul says "in every circumstance" (literally "everywhere and in all things") he is free and sufficient in Christ to care about other people's eternal well-being before his own physical and emotional needs.

Years ago a friend who was a missionary in Ecuador wrote and told me about the fabulous flowers that grew in abundance around their missionary buildings. "Why, today I even saw an orchid on a garbage pile," she said.

F.B. Meyer said, "We can do a lot to elaborate the faculty of contentment; the germ of it is in our hearts by the grace of God, but the flower and fruit demand our constant heed." That's a tall order when we are in a prison of our own making or a victim of other people's sin—but then Paul reminds us: "We can do everything through Him who gives us life," even grow flowers of contentment on a garbage pile!

# chapter two

# Plan B
## *Contentment*

Learn how to accept
the inevitable changes in life.

*Ingrid Lawrenz, MSW*

The Garden of Eden was God's perfect "Plan A." In the beginning all was good. Humanity was in perfect unity with God, other people, and even the natural world. God walked in the garden with Adam and Eve. There was no pain and no conflict. But they desired their own plan. They wanted power and control, but they got disappointment and disconnection instead.

The Romans 8:28 says, "in all things God works for the good of those who love him." He rescued us from our own best-laid plans. He gave us Jesus as a way back to His "Plan A" with a re-creative plan for a new heaven and earth. In the meantime, due to the frustrations of all creation by sin, we have to continually create "Plan Bs" in our lives.

We long for and hope for perfect unity in our churches, children who are problem free, spouses who never disappoint us, and the fulfillment of all our dreams. Hope is essential—but character and peace are built when present difficulties force us into a resilient, creative "Plan B" mode. A key way of experiencing contentment in our lives is learning how to develop and accept the inevitable changes from what we expect in life.

Karen, a mother of three, married her high school sweetheart after they both graduated from Bible college. They had plans for doing ministry together. Karen always thought she'd be well provided for and could depend on Jim for direction. She was going to be the supportive, happy wife. However, Jim developed some health problems. He started neglecting church activities and was dangerously close to addictive behaviors. His career was on-again, off-again, with a poor salary and benefits. Gradually he became depressed and withdrawn.

Karen was overly focused on Jim, trying to convince him to change and to "fix" him. Her own life was boring and their kids were showing behavior problems in school. She never thought her life would be like this. She had a choice to make. She could stick with "Plan A" and keep demanding he change no matter how bitter or sad her own life became—taking the kids down with her—or develop a "Plan B." "Plan A" was to depend on a man to take care of her and meet her needs. "Plan B" was to discover what strengths and abilities God had given her to use.

Karen chose to keep praying for "Plan A" but move on to "Plan B" because she knew she was responsible before God for her own life. She found a job in sales to help support the family, chose to attend church even if her husband didn't, and volunteered for a ministry with the disabled. Karen never dreamed she'd be a working mother or that she could socialize without Jim.

Moving on to "Plan B" helped Karen and her family. The kids started to take on more responsibility at home, appearing more secure at the same time. Her own self-confidence increased, and she was delighted to feel happy again. Even Jim withdrew less as he felt less pressure to perform, and the communication in their marriage deepened.

"Plan Bs" will look different in everyone's life, but we all are challenged to face them at one time or another. Our ability to adjust and allow God to teach us through them will lead to a life of peace and contentment.

There are plenty of "Plan A" expectations in our lives—for instance, wanting

> ### Life Lifters
>
> "*We* must learn to cultivate the virtue of contentment—which frees us from forever wanting to exist in just one stage of life."
>
> **—Lindsey O'Connor—**

to be the perfect ministry wife, to be extroverted, socially sophisticated, great at up-front activities, and gifted in music and organization. However, if that is not the kind of person you are, you can't remake your personality. "Plan B" develops as you accept yourself for whom God made you to be, discovering your gifts, and concluding that this was "Plan A" all along.

"Plan A" is to have a sunny, active, outdoor vacation. "Plan B" is adjusting when the days turn out rainy by staying inside and learning how to relax and bond as a family. "Plan A" is to have a warm, delightful "family night," while "Plan B" is to learn to control your temper when constant arguments ensue.

No one plans or prefers to have a child with

severe learning disabilities, regularly ruined plans due to bouts of migraine headaches, a spouse who is verbally cruel, being forced to leave a ministry, or a twenty-five-year marriage end in an unwanted and unexpected divorce. People can become angry, bitter, and even lose faith following a loss or when their hopes and expectations are not met. Circumstances like these can seemingly ruin your life or make you feel like a helpless victim. You can dig in your heels refusing to be happy until the problem is fixed—and you will be unhappy—or you can seek to find contentment in a "Plan B."

The apostle Paul said he had learned to be content in all circumstances, and his "Plan A" certainly did not include shipwrecks, imprisonment, or beatings!

When "Plan A" fails, we feel a loss of control. Many come to a point of saying "I never imagined my life ending up this way." It can also lead to a loss of purpose or direction and even severe depression. Developing a "Plan B" with God helps us with both control and purpose. At this point, a time of grieving is often needed. Grieving is the agonizing, soul-wrenching work of adjusting to a loss. Grieving may be brief following a disappointment or take years following a death or divorce. People vary greatly in how much time they need to grieve.

Re-creative hope might start with a prayer like this:

*Lord Jesus, I am so sad and angry about this situation. It was not in my plans for things to turn out this way. I know You are not causing it in order to punish me, nor was it in Your plan for any of us to have to deal with this kind of pain. Thank You for hearing and understanding my feelings.*

*Please help me to have the courage to change the things I can change.*

*Please help me to let go, forgive if I need to forgive, and move on when I know I've done all I can. Lord, if my expectations are the only thing I have in my control to change, help me let go of those expectations.*

*Please help me to live with disappointments, but not become disappointed with all of life. I need Your help, Lord, with a new plan so I can live well, see what is good, learn, grow, and minister. What purpose do You want my life to be about now? Please give me Your wisdom and strength. Amen.*

With a renewed attitude, you can begin to write out an inventory of options, choices, spiritual gifts, resources, likes, dislikes, and changes that need to be made.

Practicing coming up with creative "Plan Bs" for the little changes will develop a godly contentment and character that will help us cope with major "Plan A" disappointments. We can do this because we know God's ultimate "Plan A" is our future hope.

# chapter three

# Learn How to Accept
# *God's Smaller*
# Assignments

Do you ever wonder why you can't do something
grander for the Lord?

*Martha J. Konitzer*

*I* am one of those people who dreams big! In grade
school I was determined to become the first female
Evel Knievel. As a teenager I dreamed of making it big in
New York City as a singer. In college I became an over-
achiever. When a six-page paper was due, I turned in thirteen pages. As my relationship grew in Christ, I knew all
those dreams were rather silly. The only thing that really
mattered was kingdom building for Christ. So as I neared
college graduation, I decided to be a media missionary
in Tanzania, Africa.

My bubble burst when I realized that God had
some rather ordinary plans for me. Instead of Africa,
God made it clear that I was to work at a local TV
station. A few years into my career, when I was
determined to be a big TV director, God then
instructed me to marry this Christian guy who came
strutting into my life unannounced. Two years later, I
was thrust into motherhood. And then the Lord

instructed me to quit my job in TV to become a homemaker. Now I have three children whom I homeschool—not exactly what I would consider to be a dreamy, adventurous lifestyle!

There are many days when I wrestle with this bottled-up potential that is always threatening to pop and spray out all over the place. I constantly remind the Lord that His Word says the harvest is ripe and the workers are few! I beg the Lord to use me like a school girl who is constantly raising her hand with excitement as if to say, *Pick me! Pick me!* The Lord so many times says, *Yes, Martha, I see your hand. Put it down and stay right where you are. I'm going to use someone else for this task.* Then He seems to pick some average, outwardly unimpressive guy who doesn't have half the charisma or drive that I have!

After our first daughter was born, I thought God was finally going to give me the desires of my heart. He called my husband into full-time ministry. After three years of school, God sent us to a little church in Minnesota. I enjoyed being a ministry wife, but somehow, life had become a bit too comfortable. We lived in a small town, had a big house, and were ministering to mostly believers who didn't feel that they needed to be taught much of anything. I still longed to live on the edge and do something grander for the Lord.

After three years, God led us to the greater Chicago area to join a church-planting team. Starting a church from scratch would no doubt be adventurous! Immediately my mind began racing, thinking about all the *big* things we could do to reach people for Christ. Once again, however, things didn't work out as I expected. Within a short time, the team fell apart, and we were left dangling without any clear direction. My husband sent out resumes to all kinds of churches, but God closed every door. Disappointingly, my husband went back into a sales career, and I found myself raising my hand again and yelling out, *Lord! The harvest is ripe and the workers are few! We'll go anywhere! Pick us!*

After months of God's silence and much frustration on my part, I snuck upstairs and locked myself in our walk-in closet. There I proceeded to let God have it with all my bottled up anger. Then I dropped to the floor and wept. Still God was quiet but very present. I felt His hand of comfort, but He spoke no words of hope.

The next night I went for a long walk. As I walked down the long blocks, I whispered, *Lord, why won't You send us to a place where we can be used?* I waited and walked. I thought about how Billy Graham had spent his life on the cutting edge of God's work. Then I began to envy the fictitious character Christy and how she got to minister to mountain children. And then there was Amy Carmichael and Elisabeth Elliot ....

Suddenly my thoughts were interrupted. God broke His silence. *And why do you want to do big things in my name Martha? Is it for your glory, or mine?* I pondered for a moment, and then responded, *Well, I just want to know that I'm making an impact for the kingdom. Is that so wrong? You know I've tried to follow You each step of the way—but now here we are, stuck in Illinois and going nowhere. I'm disillusioned Lord. I'm confused. I feel beaten down.*

I stopped talking and listened again for God's response. Silence. I began to give God a bit more insight: *I just want You to let me in on the adventure of seeing people come to Christ! Take Jim Elliot, for example. You sent him to minister to Indians ....*

At that moment God seemed to cut me off short, responding: *Martha! I am not asking you to minister to Indians .... or go to Africa, or even to be a ministry wife right now. You are on a mission field in Illinois, and there are hurting people right in your own subdivision!*

I wrinkled my nose at God's boring assignment. Illinois didn't bring tingles to my spine, and anyone could do what He was requiring of us. Besides, Scott and I had already penetrated our subdivision. For months we had been working hard to build relationships with many of our neighbors. Since we lived in a very transient area, most of them had moved away just as we were beginning to develop friendships. We had made flyers and hand delivered them to all 150 houses in our subdivision promoting a weekly community Bible study. We stepped out in faith and forked over the money to rent a rec room belonging to the apartment complex down the street. I made cupcakes and Scott prepared the Bible study materials. The first night ... no one came.

We tried again. This time we returned to each home in the subdivision and personally knocked on doors inviting people to come to the weekly Bible study. That week a family of five came, and over many months, the group only grew to eight. I began to complain again. *See Lord, we aren't making an impact here! Nothing is happening! Can't you send us to a ripe harvest somewhere else? After all, Your Word says ....*

*I know what My Word says Martha,* the Lord interrupted. *And what kind of harvest were you looking for? An easy one? Harvesting is hard work, and sometimes it takes years to gather.* Then I sensed God's grin. He was encouraging me! *Martha, you are living on the edge. It takes an adventurous spirit to knock on doors. It takes a person with passion to work at building relationships with unbelieving neighbors. Are the people in Africa any more important than the people in Illinois? Don't underestimate your task, child. For now, I want you here.*

I thought a moment about God's perspective. I began to reflect on what we *had* accomplished in the past seven months after moving to Illinois. God allowed us to meet the physical needs of three families in our neighborhood. Scott was able to share Christ in the secular workplace with several coworkers and clients. I had opportunities to tell two women about Jesus just before they moved out of the subdivision. My six-year-old daughter told three of her friends about Jesus. And eventually, those eight people who were coming to our neighborhood Bible study came to church with us. God was bringing to mind all the small deeds we had done in order to minister to people. In His loving way, God was putting His stamp of approval on all the things I deemed petty.

As I rounded the final corner of my walk that night, God made one final point. *Martha, you don't have to die for me like Peter, you simply have to die to yourself every day.* His words split my pride into pieces. God spoke no more that night. He didn't have to. I knew what He meant. I was so eager to be the Indiana Jones of the Christian community, doing daring, adventurous things for God, but God was affirming that "being" is more important than "doing." Being totally submitted to Christ—dying to self—was just as big as dying a physical death like missionary Jim Elliot who was killed by Indians, or Peter who was martyred for his strong faith in Christ.

The following morning, while reading my Bible, the Lord confirmed His message to me. The passage burned with truth. After Jesus asked Peter "Do you love me?" for the third time, Jesus then gave Peter a glimpse into his future. He said, "'When you are old you will stretch out your hands, and someone else will dress you and lead you where you do not want to go.' Peter turned and saw John following behind them and he asked Jesus, 'Lord, what about him?' Jesus answered, 'If I want him to remain alive until I return, what is that to you? You must follow me'" (John 21:21-22).

The moment Peter is told a bit about his calling, he begins to compare himself to John. I was doing the same thing! I envied those who were in foreign lands, ministering to people who were hungry for the

Gospel. But Jesus was saying to Peter, and He was saying to me, *It doesn't matter what others are doing. Just make sure you are following Me!* Sometimes dying to self is tougher than dying a martyr's death, for there is no glory in it. But I find that God is often unimpressed with those of us who try to make big splashes in life. He is glorified when we are content to make small ripples along life's way. As for Africa? Well, I'm planning a ten-day mission trip. But for now, God has moved us again. We live in Racine, Wisconsin, where my husband is pastoring a small church. I still have big dreams, but I have learned to be content with the small ways God chooses to use me as I obediently walk with Him.

# chapter four

# "And To
# *Think*
# I Almost Missed It ...

... because of the carpeting!"
*Shelly Esser*

did it. I finally mustered up the courage, swallowed my huge pride, and invited some of the ladies from our wealthy church over for dessert. What should have been a simple task became an overwhelmingly huge barrier for me. But why? I had never felt this way about opening up my home before. But now for the first time, things I never noticed, like the size of our tiny, studio apartment clothed with worn furniture and homely fluorescent-green shag carpeting, began paralyzing my efforts. How could I invite these women, who lived in one of the wealthiest communities in the country and whose homes were literally palaces, into our miniature apartment?

Discontentment started plaguing my soul. All I had to do was walk downtown or around the block to see 3,500-plus square foot homes glaringly reminding me of what I didn't have. And almost without warning, I found myself coveting their homes, their possessions, and their lifestyles. Why did we have to find a meager apartment in a place like this during our seminary years? And how could I ever minister in a place so foreign to my own upbringing?

Paul tells us in Philippians 4:12-13, "I have learned the secret of being content in *any* and *every* situation, whether well fed or hungry, whether living in plenty or want. I can do everything through Him who gives me strength." Contentment is defined as "happy enough with what one has or is; not desiring something more or different; a satisfaction with one's possessions, position, status, or situation." It's not so much having what we want as it is wanting what we have. True contentment is being able to say, regardless of the circumstances, "I am happy right here where God has me." Paul takes it a step further using it to refer to a divinely bestowed sufficiency, *whatever* the circumstances. Especially in today's materialistic society, this is a tall order.

But Paul doesn't leave us with only the realization that we need to be content; he wonderfully tells us the "secret." It is the union with the living, exalted Christ that enables us to be content. It is being in constant touch with Him and leaning on His strength—a strength that makes it possible in every conceivable circumstance, everywhere, and in all things to be at peace, enabling us then to get on with it. This was the source of Paul's abiding strength, and it can be ours.

As we realize that it is God who is ordering all of our circumstances, whether we have little or much, and that He knows what's best for us at all times, we can begin to become content wherever He places us.

While I learned to be content in my surroundings, a remarkable thing happened: God took my focus off my *littleness* and shifted it to the *muchness* He wanted to accomplish in my apartment. When I opened the door of my home to the women God was sending my way, He made it a holy sanctuary. Endless hours were lent to counseling friends, crying, and praying with others through struggling marriages as well as sharing the love of Christ and developing deep friendships. God was revealing to me that you don't have to be rich in earthly possessions to be rich in Christ, and you don't have to have a lot to give all you have.

Particularly in ministry, where the budget is often stretched to the limit, it's easy to enviously look at all the things that are out of our reach, and even at others who may *seem* to have it better or easier than ourselves. Nothing so hinders us in ministry as longing for something else. If our thoughts and hopes are always somewhere else, it is impossible for us to truly set our hearts on the work required of us here and now.

Maybe it's not your home that's breeding a discontented heart. Maybe it's painful circumstances, an insufficient salary, an unaffordable vacation, or an unfulfilling ministry position. Whatever it is, ask God to help you discover the *secret*. He desires to give you all the strength you need to live a contented life.

Though those days in that tiny apartment were difficult for me, I am thankful for all God taught me. It's not the wallpaper or the beautifully tailored drapes of a home that is important, but rather what happens there and what God is allowed to do. And often He'll begin when we start learning to be content. The exciting thing about God is that He doesn't need a specific decor to enter a home, He just needs a willingness. And I guarantee you, He doesn't even *notice* the carpeting!

Many years have passed now, but I often find my thoughts wandering back longingly to that little one-room apartment. Those were some of the best years of my life. Interestingly, when my friends and I reminisce, the carpeting and worn furniture are never mentioned. Instead it's the tears God wiped, and the encouragement, strength, and the gift of friendship He gave us that we most remember.

And to think I almost missed it because of the carpeting!

# chapter five

# How I Became
## Satisfied
## with Less

### Debra White Smith

During the latter half of my childhood, my family was poor. My father started pastoring a small church, and the parsonage didn't have much. Our basic needs were met. Food. Water. Clothing. Shelter. In contrast, my peers were lavished with material possessions. This caused me to make one firm decision. I would be a wealthy adult. Period.

By the time I was twenty, if you gave me three nickels, I could save four. I began hoarding my money. What I didn't hoard, I spent on status items that would bring me recognition among my peers and give me feelings of worth. Nice cars, diamond rings, designer clothing, fancy furniture. We were at middle income level, but I felt smug in my materialistic accomplishments and "arrived" at church every Sunday ready to impress anyone who noticed my possessions.

Despite my smugness, I heard an inner voice that demanded more purchases, more money, more luxury to fill an ever-increasing void.

I also heard a softer voice—one that whispered there must be more to life than materialism. That softer voice led me on a journey that revolutionized my life. This journey began when I was thirty-one years old, when I began to regularly and seriously seek God, not just through obligatory prayers that had characterized my former devotional time, but by actually seeking God.

My "altar" was my bathtub—the only place I could go to escape my toddler. Leaving my husband in charge, I went into the bathroom, locked the door, and sat on the side of the bathtub almost every night. I read Scripture and sought God. "Please, God, I want to see You moving in my life," I prayed one whole autumn. Changes began to take place within me. God led me into confession, repentance, restitution, and righteousness.

I was surprised by contentment! He also led me down a path I never anticipated. During a church service, I began to feel the overwhelming urge to give half of what I made from my career as a writer to those in need. I resisted that feeling with a vengeance. After that service, I convinced myself that I had been half-crazy to even have such a thought. Between my husband's job and my writing career, we were still middle income, so giving more than my tithe shouldn't even have been an issue.

I scrapped the whole idea. But it came back again and again every time I was in church. Through daily living, I stifled the feeling that I should give sacrificially, but I could not stifle that feeling in church. To top it off, one Bible verse haunted me, "Sell all that you have and distribute to the poor, and you will have treasure in heaven; and come, follow Me" (Luke 18:22, NKJV). If God asked me to give everything I owned to the poor, would I obey?

I enjoyed my stuff too much to sacrifice it for anybody. I began to realize, sitting there on the side of my bathtub, that perhaps I wouldn't see God, really see Him, until He meant more to me than my material possessions and money. That haunting voice that had led me into seeking God confirmed my realization.

I began to fight these feelings. If I started giving sacrificially, if I started prioritizing the needs of the poor in my heart, I would have to say "no" to some of my materialistic wants and dreams. I would have to totally change my thought patterns. I would have to deny that voice within that said the more I owned, the more worthy I would be. No more luxury car, no more fancy home, furniture or clothing, no more diamonds. The notion almost sent me into a tailspin.

My husband and I were planning an international adoption. God began whispering to me to give away my adoption fund. Would I be willing to help other couples adopt children and deny my own dreams of adoption? Those other orphans couldn't be as important as the child we would adopt. Then I learned of a Russian orphanage that was struggling to keep the electricity and phone connected. Would I dare delve into the money I had hoarded to meet the needs of children I would probably never see?

After an intense, internal struggle, I did it. This decision began my journey from materialistic selfishness to selflessness. After several instances of sacrificial giving, I put up less resistance to that overwhelming, supernatural urgency that I should give until it hurt. By then, my "bathtub devotions" had moved to the couch. In my heart, I was on my face before God when I told Him I would give what He said, when He said, to whom He said.

This resulted in some radical action. I remembered Luke 3:11, "He who has two tunics, let him give to him who has none" (NKJV). This is 50-percent giving. After another vicious struggle, I gave away half of my beloved wardrobe to a friend who had prayed for clothing. These were the status clothes I had worn—the designer clothing, my absolute favorites, the items I most likely would never be able to replace because of my new standard of giving. The act of giving them was like having my insides ripped out. But God showed me that when I had given things I didn't want or need to someone less fortunate, I was not giving—I was discarding.

> **LifeLifters**
>
> "*Contentment shall come into our hearts only as we look at our life as a gift from God; we shall then be able to dance the routine of our daily household tasks or the toughness of our ministry.*"
>
> —**Soula Isch**—

After the wardrobe purge, I still had a closet full of clothing. My need—not my want—for clothing was met.

I was content with that. According to Mother Teresa, "You must give what will cost you something. This, then, is giving not just what you can live without but what you can't or don't want to live without. Then your gift becomes a sacrifice which has value before God."

Soon, I began to be spiritually nauseated by the

diamonds on my fingers. Every time I wore them, I could only think, "I let my husband waste thousands of dollars on rings that have no use except satisfying my greed and impressing others."

I began to think about the millions of children who have no food, clothing, shelter, education, or medical care. Who was I to hoard luxuries when human beings in my own city lacked necessities? I stopped wearing the diamonds.

What started as my "bathtub" search for God opened my eyes to see needs in new ways and in many places—all around me at church, in my neighborhood, in my family, overseas. I began giving on a higher level. God began a marvelous, deep work in me. I awoke one day to realize I was truly contented with my middle-income home. I was contented with my used economy car. I was excited about the prospect of sacrificially giving to feed the hungry, to educate the poor, to help the blind see. Furthermore, I felt more worthy than I had ever felt.

Materialism is a universal problem. A missionary to Africa was asked to relate the biggest problem he saw among the tribes. He replied, "Materialism. If one villager gets a new roof on his hut, his neighbors writhe with envy until they can acquire a new roof."

Christ has not called us to accumulate things for ourselves. He has called us to sacrifice our wants for the needs of others. While some Christians lead materialistic lifestyles, thousands around the world suffer from malnutrition, blindness, disease, and premature death. According to Alan Harkey, president of Christian Blind Mission International, "Each year an estimated 500,000 children go blind, primarily due to malnutrition. More than half of these children die within two years of losing their sight." For the cost of three Vitamin-A tablets—seventy-five cents—a child's blindness can often be prevented. Even so, 500,000 children go blind every year.

There is a vast difference between having a Christian belief system and living for Christ. Christ said, "If anyone desires to come after Me, let him deny himself, and take up his cross, and follow Me" (Matt. 16:24, NKJV). Denying ourselves replaces the blare of consumerism with a melody of holiness.

After we lose ourselves and our possessions completely to Him, we will find ourselves (Matt. 10:39). We find our worth in Him.

# chapter six

# Waves, Desert Islands, *and Brownies!*

Finding contentment when forced to take
a leave of absence from ministry.

*Jody Bormuth*

*I*t was a dream come true. I had been invited to join the youth ministry staff as the first girls-only director. My main job description permitted the freedom to train, equip, disciple, counsel, and teach the females of our adult youth staff, our college interns, and the students of three major area high schools. What a joy! The guys I worked with were great. The girls were passionate and eager. The ministry was bearing fruit with students receiving Christ, serving in leadership, and many moving into full-time missions or ministry positions. It felt like God and I were surfing the crest of a wondrous and exhilarating ocean wave.

Prior to and part of this crested wave was the care of our parents. Twenty-four years ago, my husband and I had become primary caretakers for his mother due to health issues and a divorce. Two years after accepting the youth ministry position, we added my father who came to live on our property in an apartment of his own. Though he had been diagnosed with kidney failure and had been slightly weakened, he was generally healthy. While Dad waited for his listing as a transplant candidate, the doctors prescribed dialysis treatments. He drove himself to and from the center. All seemed in order and I was contentedly enjoying my ministry, caring for my dad, overseeing my mother-in-law's care, and praising the Lord for His abundant life.

However, quietly, persistently a small voice began to whisper to me. "You'll need more time to care for your father." I wanted to ignore and deny the voice, but eventually I knew I needed to pray about it. I did so reluctantly. I finally asked God to make His will clear to me, and within a week I had His answer. My dad took a fall and couldn't stand up. We were not there to help him. When we discovered him, he was sore and badly shaken, but miraculously all right. Suddenly, it became clear to me what God's will was. My wondrous wave came crashing down around me.

The next day I walked into my youth pastor's office handing in my resignation. Several key pastors had also just moved away, so I was advised to keep my leaving quiet and unofficial. It was good advice, but it meant that I was allowed no formal good-bye, which would have helped me find closure. Over a period of six weeks, I simply and quietly stopped my involvement. Not only had my wave crashed, but it deposited me on the shore of a deserted island, feeling alone and abandoned. I wailed, "Here I am Lord … giving up my ministry, facing the chronic long-term care of both my mother-in-law and my father. I must now drive him to and from dialysis three times a week and confront him constantly because he stubbornly refuses to obey the doctors. To add to my duties, I now need to dispense his medications daily."

"Why me?" Companion to my wailing was the concern that comes with determining the safest care for a semi-invalid who is not cooperative, plus overseeing my mother-in-law in her assisted-care facility. My wailing led to grumbling as I read Philippians 4:11. It may say that one "learns to be content whatever the circumstances," but mine were multiplying. I was riding a different kind of wave now, a tidal wave. It swept me along, and with it came anger over giving up my beloved ministry, hurt over the inability to properly say good-bye, grief over the loss of fellowship with friends on staff and students, and worthlessness at being set on the "foot-washing, behind-the-scenes, servanthood shelf." My heart and mind told me that this was my ministry now, but a restlessness seeped in.

The dictionary defines discontent as "unsatisfied; a restless desire for something more." This reflected me perfectly. My angry wave grew as these questions swam in my mind: How was I to find contentment or satisfaction when it felt like less? How were these desires for wanting things back the way they were ever going to leave? The phrase, "learn to be content" rolled around in my head. It haunted me. It wouldn't let me enjoy my discontent. I cried out to God. "Okay! Teach me! Show me! I'm listening. Please give me something to hold onto during all of this!"

His answer mystified me. "Contentment is like eating brownies with no icing!" Surely I was mistaken and heard it wrong. What kind of handle was that? I turned it over and over in my mind. I meditated on it. I read the Scriptures. I went on walks. Slowly God revealed to me that to learn contentment was to be satisfied with what I already had—nothing more, nothing less. It seemed too simple. Yet simple was what I needed—simple, like a plain brownie, no icing!

You see, brownies are my favorite chocolate snack. If a plain brownie is all I have to eat, I am content. I can enjoy it completely. Now if it happens that someone comes along and ices my brownie, it's a nice perk. But then what if someone comes along and removes my icing? For a true brownie lover, it's no problem because I still have my brownie. For me, learning contentment was the revelation that Jesus Christ "in me" was and is like this brownie. Circumstances and people may come into my life and may add icing (my ministry for example). I don't have to like it when the icing is removed, but regardless, I have my relationship with Christ. I had forgotten that. Truly I had taken Him for granted. According to Colossians 1:27 the truth is, "Christ in me ... the hope of glory." I compared this basic truth with my present "angry wave, desert-island, no icing" circumstances.

Dr. Larry Crabb in his book *The Marriage Builder* made his own comparison. He states that in Jesus' day there were those who tore their clothes to show anguish at difficult circumstances versus the priests who were forbidden to tear their clothes. He writes, "The answer lies in a privilege accorded only to the priests. None but the high priest knew what it was to stand in the presence of the Holy Place. Only he could approach God and live. Now, compare his privilege of access with his responsibility not to tear his robe. The lesson is clear: Someone who has access to the immediate presence of God never has reason to regard anything as a disaster. When a person is aware of God's presence in his or her own life, nothing that happens need provoke a sense of despair. To do so implies God is impotent to work for eternal good in our set of circumstances." God taught me that I had been tearing my robe, demanding icing for my brownie, and declaring that Jesus was not enough. My grumbling had betrayed my lack of gratitude for access to the very throne room of God.

When the full impact of that truth soaked in, the angry, grumbling wave hit shore and fizzled into frothy foam and slowly dissipated. My plain brownie was adequate and my desert island bloomed. I clung to Jesus as all I needed. He led me to see my dad and mother-in-law with eyes of renewed compassion. The "foot-washing" became easier. I found myself turning their care into a positive challenge each day, though I still missed the ministry and the students. Despite an uncertain future and the recurrent waves of emotions provoked by my new "ministry," an unmistakable growing contentment became a calming, restful sea within. I felt "kept" in His hands, safe and warm. Christ blessed me with the sweet private satisfaction that comes from having continuous access to *Him*.

What is keeping you from contentment in Christ alone whether in an official ministry or not? What icing do you desire more than the throne room of God? Are there any angry tidal waves in your life right now? When will this privilege we constantly share with Him be enough? When will you allow your island to bloom? I had to learn what the Webster's dictionary already knew about being content: "happy enough with what one is or has, not desiring more or different; satisfied."

# chapter seven

# The Other
# *Woman*

## *Jackie Oesch*

*T*he keynote speaker asked the audience of pastors and their wives a question that made me want to jump up out of my chair: What is the most difficult aspect of ministry? Oh, I knew the answer to that question! I wanted to shout it out. The most difficult aspect of ministry was learning to live with his "mistress."

I remember well the day we arrived in San Antonio eager to begin ministry at our small church on the southside. Quickly our private life as husband and wife was invaded by an invisible intruder that was burrowing its way into our newly established home. Norb was involved in the work he was called to do and preoccupied with ministry responsibilities, and he was unaware of what I was discovering about our life together.

I could not pinpoint what was happening. I only knew Norb was no longer all mine. He would leave early in the morning all showered and fresh (dressed with a clean shirt and pressed slacks, smoothly shaven face) and with the alluring aroma of aftershave. With a quick kiss he was out the door yelling over his shoulder something about looking forward to being home for dinner but that he had a meeting at seven.

What could I say? Pastors were *supposed* to be busy. They were often needed at a moment's notice. His life was not his own. Of course, he was excited about finally doing the work the seminary had trained him to do. As for me, well, I considered these early days a necessary phase—all part of adjusting to my new role as "the pastor's wife."

It didn't take long for me to discover what this "mistress" was like. She was extremely presumptuous. She demanded his time and his energy which meant that he would come home late at night tired and exhausted. She monopolized his thoughts so when I would ask him to share what he was thinking, he usually responded with something pertaining to her. In bed at night his final comments reflected his concern for her health and well being. She seemed to have his permission to invade our privacy any time—day or night. She took him out of town for conventions and speaking engagements. Life in a parsonage meant that she dictated the home in which we lived and even determined when the repairs would be completed. She ran our home and our relationship. Because of her we found ourselves giving each other the leftovers of our lives.

What did this do to me? I was a jealous woman; I became resentful and bitter toward them and their relationship. With every passing day, I grew more and more discontent with our life. I could not get rid of her, and I was not about to compete with her. I found myself closing off my feelings. I wasn't going to let the intimacy they were sharing continue to hurt me. I felt I was being robbed of something that was mine. It was painful to realize that Norb *chose* to nurture this relationship and encouraged it to continue. He seemed to stand for her, justifying her position within our marriage.

By turning my anger inward I allowed waves of depression to invade my life. I was struggling to cope with what was happening. Divorce was out of the question, and yet the loneliness and separation seemed unbearable. Another big problem was guilt. How could I possibly resent the fact that Norb was spending his time and energy doing "the Lord's work?"

The relationship persisted. She continually encouraged him by giving him strokes of love and gratitude for all that he had done for her by ministering to her at such critical times. She would tell him how meaningful sermons and Bible studies had been which caused him to strive to do better and to do more. He would be encouraged as she grew in size and burdened by her as she grew in needs.

My guilt intensified as church members would share with me how fortunate I was to be married to such a "man of God." They would insist on sharing with me how loving, caring, and considerate he was, how knowledgeable he was of Scripture, and how eager he was to visit with them in their home. Their compliments compounded my guilt and provided fuel for my anger. My depression continued. How was I ever to compete with God?

After eight and a half years in San Antonio we accepted a call to a growing congregation in

Bakersfield, California. Our family with two children soon grew to a family with four. Life as a mother was demanding. The children consumed my time and energy, and I found myself directing my feelings into constructive time with them. They became my friends. We understood and accepted each other. We enjoyed one another's company. I wanted to spend time with them. My periods of depression became less frequent. I allowed the children to fill the intense void I felt as a result of Norb's preoccupation with the demands of pastoral ministry.

About ten years into our marriage Norb decided to begin his doctoral program. I became involved in the program as a member of his required advisory board. I found the discussions regarding ministry challenging and stimulating. However, the assignment that brought about the biggest revelation for me was the question: What is *your* ministry? As I wrestled with this question I was forced to identify those in my life whom the Lord had called me to serve, those to whom by meeting their needs God enabled me to bring the Gospel, namely Jesus Christ. I began to recognize that both Norb and I had specific and unique ministries. I was challenged to identify and accept not only my ministry, but Norb's also.

God was busy teaching me many things during this period of my life. I began to understand the concept of ministry. I had been reacting to his ministry as his "mistress," until I realized that I was also in ministry! No longer did I find myself fellowshipping with discontentment or competing with a "mistress" but rather participating in a ministry with Norb. By changing my attitude the Lord brought me from resentment of a "mistress" to the love and excitement of a ministry. Together we would be able to reach out to serve.

I began to understand that Norb was part of the ministry God had given me. I looked for ways of caring for his needs in order that he might better function in his ministry. I realized that by feeding and caring for him, by being attentive to him and loving him, I was developing a sense of satisfaction and contentment which came from knowing that I was doing ministry specifically designed by God for me. I was beginning to understand the same to be true regarding our children, the women who gathered with me for Wednesday morning Bible study, and for members of the congregation with their countless needs.

Today life is exciting. Saying "yes" or "no" to opportunities is determined by the specific ministry which is mine. Ministry enables me to be Jesus to the world around me, the ministry of bringing the good news of the Gospel to those I am called to serve.

# chapter eight

# What's My *Story?*

*Julie White Norton*

*"I remembered my frustration at going alone
to the beach on my last vacation.
How was I feeling about my singleness?
Most any day, that is a loaded question."*

y dear friend took off her sunglasses, cocked her head to the side and asked me, "So how are you feeling about your singleness these days?" I thought of the black oil I had recently spilled on my carport as I tried to fix my broken lawnmower. A limited budget and the lack of a husband had left this dirty task in my incapable hands. I thought of the myriad of wedding invitations that were addressed Julie and "guest." Is it appropriate to take a parakeet to a wedding? I remembered my frustration at going alone to the beach on my last vacation. How was I feeling about my singleness? Most any day, that is a loaded question.

My friend who asked the question is a super mother of four great kids. She has a sweet marriage to a pastor. Her week is loaded with juggling needs. A few days before our conversation she had stayed up half the night with a sick child. I recalled her year and a half of terror dealing with the drug problem of another one of her children. She would probably love to have a date with a lawnmower or a chance to escape to the beach alone with God.

I highly value contentment. I strive to live a balanced life filled with gratitude to God for the blessings of my singleness and prayerful honesty about many unmet preferences. I think it's possible to cultivate a grateful heart even when your prayers for a mate seem to run forward like the yellow highway lines on a flat horizon.

I've seen some bitter, single Christian women in my life. Some have developed a sharp sense of hatred for all males. Some, longing to be married, have taken matters into their own hands and regret it. Others have placed their whole life on hold as they sit by the phone and wait for "Mr. Right" to dial. I've decided bitterness is not an option for me.

The secret to contentment seems to be married to (forgive the pun) developing a realistic attitude of gratitude. Some ways I've learned to help myself develop gratitude follow.

*Make friends with married people.* I like to frequent the homes of my married friends, especially the ones with kids. I often walk away thanking God for the simplicity of my single state. I once lived with a family. Do you realize that children talk in the morning? Some of them even cry before 8:00 A.M. Who has time for that?

*Acknowledge the limits of marriage.* Make a list of the times you feel most frustrated about your singleness. Talk to some of your married girlfriends. I've learned that many of them are working on lawnmowers too.

*Have "rotic" evenings.* A "rotic" evening is the same as a *romantic* evening without the man. Be sure that you are filling your life with beauty. Buy yourself flowers. Eat dinner with your friends by candlelight on china. Walk on the beach at sunset.

*Spend less time wishing and more time enjoying the freedoms of singleness.* Thank God for a full night's sleep. Have a blast with your friends on a weekend away. Take your niece home when she's crying.

How am I feeling about my singleness these days? It depends on the hour. My feelings change so often that they are not very reliable. I'm thinking that there are parts of singleness that would be hard to trade for the challenges of married life. I'm also thinking that God commands me to have an attitude of contentment regardless of who fixes my lawnmower.

Julie Norton White

# chapter nine

# Digging Deeper:
## *Cultivating*
## Contentment

### *Elizabeth Greene*

D o you remember the children's book, *Alexander and his Terrible, Horrible, No Good, Very Bad Day*? Everything that can go wrong happens to Alexander from the moment he wakes until bedtime. Alexander grumbles his way through the day. Often we find it easier to focus on the negative circumstances of life, which leads to complaining, rather than counting the blessings God has sent our way. If we are to cultivate contentment, we must chose to see the blessings in the midst of unmet expectations and difficult circumstances. Sometimes we fail to recognize God's gentle care of us—just as the Israelites did under the leadership of Moses.

The Israelites mastered the fine art of grumbling. Moses led the children of Israel out of Egypt into the desert toward the Promised Land. God had already provided for His people in amazing ways. He caused Pharaoh to let the people go, parted the Red Sea for their safe escape, and provided sweet water to quench their thirst. Then they camped near Elim and enjoyed twelve springs and seventy palm trees. Water and shade—what blessings God bestowed on them in the hot, dry desert. Do you think the people expressed joy and contentment with all of God's gracious provisions? Do you think they rejoiced that God heard their cry and led them from slavery to freedom?

*Read Exodus 16:1-3*

- What was the attitude of the Israelites?
- Where would they rather be?
- What did they miss about Egypt?

How quickly they forgot about their miserable life in Egypt. Only two-and-a-half months after departing Egypt they desired to return to a lifetime of slavery.

*Read Exodus 1:14*

- What was the Israelites' life like under Egyptian rule?

Life with God meant freedom, provision, and faith. Yet they would rather trade that to return to ruthless Egyptian slavery due to hunger! The people lacked contentment with God's provision and care. They also lacked faith that He would prove faithful in their present predicament.

If we are to cultivate an attitude of contentment, we must avoid the complaining trap of the Israelites. If they had looked back and focused on the provisions of the past, they would have found the faith to believe that God could provide for their next big challenge—hunger.

- Do you find yourself lacking contentment about a circumstance right now? It could be a marriage, family, or financial challenge.
- What ways have you seen the hand of God provide for you in the midst of this difficulty? Write them down.

• How can seeing the hand of God at work in the past give you contentment for the present?

*Read Exodus 16:11-12*

• How did God provide for His hungry people?

God did not take His people out of the desert, but He cared for their needs while there. In fact, Deuteronomy 8:4 tells us that their clothes did not wear out and their feet did not swell as they wandered in the wilderness. God met all the needs of His people on their journey to the Promised Land. Did you notice how God cared for His children? They complained that at least in Egypt they "sat by the pots of meat, when we ate bread to the full" (16:3, NASB).

> **LifeLifters**
>
> "*N*othing stays the same forever, so throughout our lives we always have an opportunity to learn to be content in whatever place or season we find ourselves."
>
> **—Lindsey O'Conner—**

• What kind of food did God give them in the desert? (16:12)

How gracious is God to give them just what they requested!

• As you wander in your own wilderness, how can you avoid the grumbling trap of the Israelites?

• How does faith in God affect your level of contentment?

*Read Psalm 78:1-39*

In this passage you will see all the ways God provided for His people and the continuing grumbling of the Israelites. How easy it is to fall into the grumbling trap! Count all the ways God provided for them on their journey. If they had focused on all God's wonders, how do you think their complaining attitude would have been affected?

An old hymn gives great advice when it comes to cultivating contentment.

## Count Your Blessings
(Johnson Oatman, Jr.)

When upon life's billows you are tempest tossed,
When you are discouraged, thinking all is lost,
Count your many blessings; name them one by one,
And it will surprise you what the Lord hath done.

So amid the conflict, whether great or small,
Do not be disheartened—God is over all,
Count your many blessings, name them one by one,
Count your many blessings, see what God hath done.

## Prayer

*Dear God,*

*Thank you for showing me that you are Jehovah Jirah, the God who provides. I pray that I will trust in You to meet all my needs in the midst of life's disappointments. Help me to count all of the blessings You have showered on me rather than to complain about my circumstances. May I learn to be content no matter what my situation, because my hope and joy rests in You alone.*

*Amen.*

# chapter ten

# Counseling Corner:
## *When More*
## Is Not Enough

*Ingrid Lawrenz, MSW*

*M*oney, or the lack of it, is a perennial problem for ministry families. It's so easy to buy into the American dream that money will bring us happiness. There's always an emotional aspect to our finances. Buying into the American dream promotes the elusive fantasy that money brings contentment, and that just a little more than what you have right now will be enough.

We often feel a hunger and emptiness that drives us. We want to fill it with more: more money, more food, more romance. However, trying to fill this desire for more, this hole, is futile. Edward, in C. S. Lewis' *The Lion, the Witch and the Wardrobe*, could never be satisfied with enough Turkish taffy. He always wanted more. Likewise, we think more will satisfy us. We feel deprived, we feel deserving, we ache, and we nervously fret for more. Some women even become severely depressed, feeling caught in a black hole of emptiness. But "enough" never comes, unless we confront the lie itself. The Bible calls this a "continual lust for more" (Eph. 4:19). Even Adam and Eve wanted more. They ate from the forbidden tree because Satan lied to them. Wanting more, they ended up with less.

This longing for more is the earthly symptom of incompleteness and sin this side of glory. It's a frame of mind more than a circumstance. The desire for more is sometimes that universal hunger for heaven, a longing for the only One who can truly fill us—God Himself. We can be satisfied, fulfilled, and content with Christ.

Of course, real financial problems are difficult, so the Bible exhorts the church to generously provide for its leaders. However, our discontent often comes when we make comparisons and when we envy. As missionaries or pastors' wives we cannot begin to compare or compete with the wealthy in our congregations. We have followed a sacrificial call into ministry. If we are angry about this, we need to take our feelings to God instead of blaming our husbands.

> ### LifeLifters
>
> "*We* can live as though Christ died yesterday, rose today, and is coming tomorrow, or we can live as though Christ died, period. We can count blessings, or we can count calamities … It's our choice."
>
> —**Barbara Johnson**—

John Stuart Mill said, "I have learned to seek my happiness not by trying to fulfill all my desires but by limiting them." What a novel idea! We need to train our appetites, not be driven by them. We're surrounded by so much stuff and so many opportunities. Most of it is good, but it's more than we can humanly afford or can fit into our schedule. Even our children are bombarded with so many sports, lessons, and activities that they can forget how to just relax and play. Limiting our expansive desires and interests can lead to peace.

Joseph Novello, in his book *The Myth of More*, says, "I desire to want what I have and not want what I do not have." Think about that—wanting what you already have—and not desiring more. Shopping, planning, and hunting for sales and coupons produces adrenaline, but returning, storing, cleaning, rearranging, and moving them all take our precious life energy. The "stuff" can control us. We can become dependent on our belongings, feeling obliged to use them and take care of them.

Challenging the myth that more makes us happy and content can lead to a reframing of our lives. "Who" is more important to us than "what." Think of what we could do with the extra time we would have if we were no longer handling so much stuff.

Practically speaking, there is peace in simplicity. A couple of nice-looking outfits are better than a stuffed closet. The bulging closet brings the stress of choosing what to wear, what fits, what matches, and what to wear occasionally to justify buying it in the first place. It may take a little humility, but is pride worth the price?

Consider borrowing or renting instead of buying. For example, renting a boat, a trailer, mountain bikes, or other things we occasionally use will not only save money but will save us hours of upkeep and storage. Ask if owning them will actually bring contentment or extra anxiety.

Jesus said He had neither a home nor bed of His own. He lived a simple life. People mattered to Him, as did doing the will of His Father in heaven. Satan tempted Him in the wilderness with the myth of more. Satan promised, "All this I will give you," he said, "if you will bow down and worship me" (Matt. 4:9). Ironically, as with all of Satan's lies, Jesus would not have gained more; He would have lost everything.

It is a blessing to have enough money to live without fear. Yet we need to be wise and discerning about what we need and what we chase after to gain happiness. The seminary years are usually a sparse and tense time of life, but it seems that as soon as the fear of survival ends, the lust for fulfilling all desires enters. It is then that credit card bills can get out of control. Debt can cause far more stress and outweigh any pleasure we may get from the things we buy.

Learning to live as a spiritual being in this physical and material world is a perennial problem. Jesus spoke to this issue when He challenged us to build up heavenly treasure that will not be destroyed by moth or rust. We need His help daily.

# chapter eleven

# *"I'm Their* Leader...

## ...which way did they go?"
## *Maggie Wallem Rowe*

*H*aven't we all felt like that at one time or another? Whether you've agreed to be the buck-stopper or the trailblazer, the pacesetter or the pathfinder, you are the one in charge. You might be the mogul of women's ministry in your church, the superintendent of the Sunday school or even the tycoon in charge of the toddlers (or the trustees!), but the challenge is the same: you feel overextended and under-equipped. You're running the race with the best of them, but you've reached a critical juncture where you're wondering where all the troops are who are supposed to be running with you.

"But I'm not a leader," you murmur. "I agreed to take on this responsibility just because it needed doing; that doesn't make me anybody's leader." Are you so sure about that?

By definition, a leader is a person who influences people to accomplish a purpose. If you are teaching that toddler to use the potty and love Jesus, or showing your teenager by example how to respect

herself and follow God, you are a leader. If you a
the one in the office that others turn to when th
need a shoulder to lean on, or a level head to adv
them, you are a leader. If you are a church meml
who spots a need and rallies others around to meet
you are a leader.

Evangelical leader, Leighton Ford, believes that
can make one of two mistakes in viewing leadersl
development, "One is to attach a mystique
leadership that says in effect, 'God calls leade
Leaders are born. There is nothing we can do about
The opposite is to say, 'Leaders are made. With t
right techniques, we can produce them.'" Ford goes
to say that it is always true that God gives leadersl
to His Church and His kingdom (Ps. 75:6-7), but it
also true that there are processes that He uses
produce His leaders, processes evident in t
Scriptures when we study the stories of Moses, Dav
and Paul.

These are the stories that I studied when I had
major decision to make four years ago. I had be
asked to accept a major leadership positi
coordinating women's ministries regionally in Ne
England. I was, in a word, terrified. Terrified of t
time it would take. Terrified of the responsibili
Terrified to even be thought of as a leader when I fi
so very immature and inadequate.

Yet when I studied the principles of leadersh
development apparent in the Scriptures, I could n
help but see the parallels. Moses felt terrib
inadequate as well; so did Gideon. The young proph
Jeremiah was well aware of his immaturity. Th
apostles Paul and Peter had personal histories th

should have disqualified them for ministry according to some contemporary standards. Yet God chose them.

I have come to realize that God will either *gift* us or *grow* us to serve in the various leadership capacities to which He calls us. To say "no" to Him might be to turn down the very experience He would have used to help us become the woman we have always wanted to be— women influencing people for a critically important purpose.

> **LifeLifters**
>
> "*We* should be content for no matter how great our need, the Divine Resources are never exhausted!"
>
> —**Anonymous**—

While none of us will develop identical leadership styles, certain characteristics of effective leadership are worth noting:

**1. Effective leadership begins with submission to the will and purposes of God.**

Dr. J. Robert Clinton writes, "Anyone can submit to something he or she wants. Submission is tested only when the thing is not desired." In speaking of surviving a time of testing, the great South African, Andrew Murray, once preached from Acts 27, concluding, "In His good time, He will bring me out again—how and when He knows. So let me say: I am (a) here by God's appointment; (b) in His keeping; (c) under His training; (d) for His time." Leadership is surely a testing.

**2. Effective leadership is not measured by how much you can accomplish alone, but by how much you can influence others to share the vision.**

Recently, I had the privilege of attending a large conference for women. With over a thousand women in attendance, the conference was a massive organizational effort indeed. When I spotted the director of women's ministries in the crowded foyer that morning, however, she was calm and serene. "I have very little to do today," Cynthia explained. "I have a wonderful group of women running everything!" That's good leadership.

**3. Effective leaders search for *strategic methods* for reaching and training people.**
You do not have to have "all the answers" yourself before you can begin to lead a group. In fact, it's best if you don't. (Who could follow in your footsteps?) Good leaders are simply committed to finding ways that will help their people grow. A wealth of excellent material on leadership development is available.

**4. Effective leaders *do not over-schedule their lives.*** In her account of living among the Amish, writer Sue Bender comments in *Plain and Simple*, "The Amish often leave a space in their day, a seeming mistake in the midst of their well-thought-out-plans, to serve as an opening to let the Spirit come in." I am learning that we dare not put our work before our worship. Leave space in your life to let the Spirit in.

**5. Effective leaders *pray for successors*.**
My ministry predecessor told me to begin praying for my replacement before I ever joined the staff. It was wonderful advice. Someone should be succeeding you in practically every leadership position you hold (unless it's as a mother!). Storm the gates of heaven on her behalf.

**6. Effective leaders enlist *personal prayer support* for their work.**

Sometimes we hesitate to ask for help out of pride or a fear of being self-aggrandizing. We need to be soberly aware that we are engaged in spiritual warfare in which the enemy often targets leaders first. It's crucial that we establish prayer bunkers. Enlist the support of others who will pray for you as you assume added responsibilities.

Above all, do not neglect your own spiritual life. Prayer will provide the power that fuels your ministry, and the reminder that this is God's work after all. As Paul encouraged the Thessalonians, "He who called you is faithful and He will do it!"

# chapter twelve

# More Is Caught
## than Taught

### *Jackie Katz*

*O*ur kids catch things, and I don't mean colds, flu, or the chicken pox. I'm talking about kids catching our values and attitudes, our faith, our very hearts. They are like blotters soaking up what they see and experience, constantly watching, evaluating, learning, and incorporating from everything we do. "More is caught than taught," John Maxwell said, "You can teach your kids what you know but you reproduce what you are."

If we want our children to catch a living, rich, vital faith that will sustain them through life, then we must own such a faith. We cannot give them what we do not possess and they cannot catch what they do not see.

Scripture captures this truth in Deuteronomy 6:5-7: "*You* shall love the LORD *your* God with all *your* heart and with all *your* soul and with all *your* might. These words, which I am commanding *you* today, shall be on *your* heart. *You* shall teach them diligently to *your* sons and shall talk of them when *you* sit in *your* house." (NASB)

It is not until *our* hearts and souls are fully committed to loving God that we can effectively teach His ways to our children when they sit in our house. We can tell our children to have a strong active belief system all day long, but if they don't see it illustrated in us, the message doesn't penetrate their hearts. Kids can easily detect hypocrites, and phonies make lousy coaches.

The practice of our faith won't be perfect, but it must be genuine. How will our children judge our faith to be genuine? In two ways:

1. By our understanding that knowledge of the Word alone just doesn't cut it. It is the daily practice of God's commandments that verifies a genuine faith.

2. By how we handle tests and trials. A genuine faith endures in the face of trials and holds fast to God's faithfulness. For our faith to have impact on our children we need to remember it is not so much *what* happens to us but *how* we handle it.

What have my children caught from me? Certainly they have observed and been disappointed by my inclination toward sin and serving the flesh. They have been witness to my struggle in "laying aside every encumbrance and the sin that so easily entangles me" and hinders my race. I tremble when I think of what my children have caught from me. It fills me with regret and a deep sadness. But I trust they have also caught my love for God and His Word, my compassion for the ministry and God's people, and my fierce love of family.

I taught my children that forgiveness was possible when they saw my husband and me grant forgiveness to a church that rejected us and slandered our good reputation. Forgiveness wasn't easy and certainly not based on feelings. We forgave because God commanded it. Both our son and daughter were attending seminary at the time, and I was gripped by the realization that they were watching how we handled difficult situations in ministry.

I taught my children that God is the Blessed Controller of all things, that He lovingly and intricately weaves together the many details of our lives. This truth was not caught until one church board reneged on their promise to allow us to move out of the parsonage and into our own home. We were all disappointed. It was hard for us to see how God was in control in this situation. It seemed that men had the upper hand. After some struggling, we decided to accept the board's decision as God's plan for us. It all became clear when in six months we were called to a new ministry.

I worked hard at teaching my son not to live by his feelings. "I don't feel like it," was his favorite expression. "It doesn't matter how you feel. Just do it!" I would reply. I know he has caught this principle because now as a youth pastor he is often heard saying to his group of junior-highers, "It doesn't matter how you feel. Just do it!"

Yes, kids catch things. They can catch our bad attitudes or imperfect manners, but they can also catch a deep passion for God, a set of convictions strong enough to carry them through any temptation, a framework of belief that they can build their lives upon. Kids catch the very essence of who we are. What are your kids catching from you?

# chapter thirteen

# A Daughter's
## Perspective—

*"... and here's what I caught!"*
### Laurie McIntyre

The view from the pew proved to be an excellent school of learning. I "caught" many life lessons as I watched from my own PK (pastor's kid) corner.

I learned that every believer, including children, can and should contribute to the body of Christ and the life of the congregation. As a little girl I asked Jesus into my heart and soon learned that I had been given special spiritual gifts to serve Him. By late elementary school Mom and Dad were helping me develop mine. Together we found bite-sized, age-appropriate service opportunities—even baking for a sick neighbor counted!

The question was often asked, "What would you like to do for Jesus this week, summer, or year?" One summer in junior high I was telling the missionary story at VBS. Later I joined the youth group planning team and taught Sunday school, all the while experiencing my own supernatural blessings as a result of serving. Ministry was not just Dad's job; it was a family endeavor! I am in ministry today because I was given opportunities to test my gifts in my parent's church.

I learned that God's Word really has the answers to life's problems. My parents took God's Word seriously. Its truths were incorporated into everyday conversation: at the dinner table, in the car, at the park, on the way home from a movie. The Bible was our grid for life. I watched it bring comfort, solve conflicts, inspire hope, and answer soul-searching questions. I saw next-door neighbors and desperately needy people transformed by the power of God's Word. It changed our home, my parents, and me. My parents' ready grasp of Scripture inspired a desire in me to know the Bible and establish my life solidly on its principles.

> ### LifeLifters
>
> " *S*pend one hour a day in adoration of the Lord Jesus and you will be all right, you will be content!"
>
> —**Mother Teresa**—

I learned that sacrifice is a part of life. In a day where God's work is often sacrificed on the altar of family, our family was sometimes sacrificed for the sake of ministry. And we survived! We learned that people's crises are not always convenient. A vacation might be shortened a day due to a parishioner's sudden death, or unexpected company had to be entertained graciously when a football game and a nap were much preferred. Such sacrifice prepared me for life's inconveniences, marriage's demands, and ministry's challenges.

I learned that forgiveness is not easy but it is essential for healing. Unfortunately, criticism runs rampant in churches and the minister's family is not left unscathed. Hurtful words, callous looks, malicious gossip, and even vicious lies can all leave deep wounds. I know because one church experience nearly left us in shreds. Anger and protective reproaches against people seemed the safest and justified reaction. Knowing their pain, I watched Mom and Dad wrestle through the hurt and ultimately do what I thought impossible; they forgave without being asked. It was volitional and real. They chose not to retaliate, not to harbor bitterness, not to rehearse the details for eager ears, not to question God's sovereignty. Their end was growth, freedom, and future ministry success. As for me, I saw that forgiveness is the beginning of the healing process, not the end. And what relationship does not need the touch of forgiveness?

It has been said that all a person needs to know is learned in kindergarten, but for me, all I needed to know was learned in the parsonage.

## Author Biographies

**Jill Briscoe** is a popular writer and conference speaker who has authored over forty books. She directs Telling the Truth media ministries with her husband, Stuart, and ministers through speaking engagements around the world. Jill is executive editor of Just Between Us, a magazine for ministry wives and women in leadership, and serves on the boards of World Relief and Christianity Today International. Jill and Stuart live in suburban Milwaukee, Wisconsin, and have three grown children and thirteen grandchildren.

**Ingrid Lawrenz, MSW** is a licensed social worker who has been counseling for seventeen years. Ingrid has been a pastor's wife for twenty-seven years and is currently the senior pastor's wife at Elmbrook Church in suburban Brookfield, Wisconsin. She and her husband, Mel, have two teenagers and lives in Waukesha, Wisconsin.

**Martha J. Konitzer** serves as a pastor's wife in Racine, Wisconsin. Martha leads a "Green Berets" women's ministry and coordinates musical productions for her church.

**Shelly Esser** has been the editor of *Just Between Us*, a magazine for ministry wives and women in leadership, for the last thirteen years. She has written numerous published articles and ministered to women for over twenty years. Her recent book, *My Cup Overflows—A Deeper Study of Psalm 23* encourages women to discover God's shepherd love and care for them. She lives in southeastern Wisconsin, with her husband, John, and four daughters.

**Debra White Smith** is the acclaimed author of such life-changing titles as *Romancing Your Husband, The Harder I Laugh, the Deeper I Hurt* (with Stan Toler), *More than Rubies: Becoming a Woman of Godly Influence* (where this chapter is excerpted from) and the popular *Seven Sisters* fiction series. Debra is also a much-sought-after conference speaker. Debra and her family live in Jacksonville, Texas.

**Jody Bormuth** has been involved in Christian service for over thirty years. Jody is on staff at her church, working in various ministries: leading Bible studies, counseling, and mentoring women of all ages. She is a recent graduate from Multnomah Biblical Seminary with a Master's degree in pastoral ministries. She and her husband, Tom, have two grown daughters and live in Grants Pass, Oregon.

**Jackie Oesch** has served with her husband, Norb, for the past thirty-two years in church ministry. Jackie is the director of the Partner Program for the Pastoral Leadership Institute in Santa Ana, California. Most recently, she has launched FullValue Ministries with the message that everyone is worth full value in Jesus. Jackie is an experienced consultant, Bible study and small group leader, and has served as director of women's ministries at St. John's Lutheran Church in both Bakersfield and Orange, California. She and her husband have four grown children and two grandchildren and live in Orange, California.

**Julie Norton White** holds a Masters of Arts and Religion degree from Trinity Evangelical Divinity School. Julie has ministered to women from Illinois to Tokyo. Her ministry focus is equipping and training Christian women for effective ministry through leadership development and mentoring. Julie and her husband, David, live in Duluth, Georgia.

**Elizabeth Greene** has an M.A. in Christian Education and formerly served as a children's ministry pastor for six years at Elmbrook Church in Brookfield, Wisconsin. Elizabeth continues to remain active in children's and women's ministries through teaching and speaking. She lives in Waukesha, Wisconsin, with her husband, Ryan, and two children.

**Maggie Wallem Rowe** recently relocated to Wheaton, Illinois, where her husband is senior pastor of First Baptist Church, after devoting twenty-five years of ministry in New England. Maggie has a national speaking ministry and evangelistic drama ministry. She is also a contributing author to a number of books.

**Jackie Katz** received her ministry training at Philadelphia Biblical University. She is an experienced teacher and communicator, biblical counselor and has been a columnist for *Just Between Us*, a magazine for ministry wives and women in leadership. She brings a mix of insight, humor, and practicality that encourages God's gift of hope and joy in all she does. She and her husband have partnered in ministry for thirty-nine years. They have two grown children and seven grandchildren and live in Spring Grove, Pennsylvania.

**Laurie McIntyre** has been motivating and inspiring women of all ages as the associate pastor of women's ministries at Elmbrook Church in Brookfield, Wisconsin. In addition, she maintains an ambitious speaking schedule at retreats and serves on the board of MOPS International. Laurie has co-authored Designing Effective Women's Ministries with Jill Briscoe and Beth Seversen and is a contributing author of *Mothers Have Angel Wings* by Carol Kent. Laurie is a graduate of Biola University and Dallas Theological Seminary. She and her husband, Bob, have two daughters.

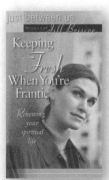

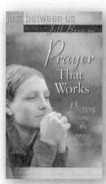

**Prayer that Works**
Plugging into the
power source.
ISBN 0-78143-953-1
ITEM #102352

Only $5.99 each!

**Resolving Conflict**
Stilling the storms of life.
ISBN 0-78143-954-X
ITEM #102353

**The Search for Balance**
Keeping first things first.
ISBN 0-78143-955-8
ITEM #102354

**Spiritual Warfare**
Equipping yourself for battle.
ISBN 0-78143-948-5
ITEM #102347